SEAN WEAFER

Invoking The Feminine

Strength, Love & Wisdom

○ SEANWEAFER.COM

*To my beautiful wife, Sharon, who has encouraged and
educated me through sharing her wonderful
conversations, her perceptive insights and personal
experiences on all things concerning the wonderful and
eternal mystery of women.*

*To my good friend and valued colleague, Gill Carrie, for
her belief, amazing support and advocacy of this book's
philosophy. Her experience as a writer and publisher
has been invaluable and greatly appreciated.*

*Lastly, to my gang of five sisters – Maire, Aine, Eileen,
Cliona, and Sinead – for all the* laughs.

Blessed am I among women.

Contents

Preface

The Journey Starts Here

In June 2011, Professors Anita Woolley and Thomas W. Malone were interviewed in the *Harvard Business Review* and produced an interesting finding from their preliminary research into group dynamics.

Their initial research had predicted that what made teams smarter, more cohesive and therefore more effective was not necessarily the introduction of smarter people. Whilst this would certainly raise the average individual IQ of team members, making teams more effective was actually achieved by raising the 'collective IQ' of the group.

But how could raising this 'collective IQ' be achieved?

The answer was interesting: add more women. And the more women added, the better, up to a point.

What mattered was 'social sensitivity' – the ability to discuss, to accept criticism, to listen with an open mind and to listen to all views before a decision was made.

The addition of womens' energies and values of engagement led to better thinking and better decision-making and therefore to better outcomes.

On reading this, I was reminded of the quote that insanity is 'doing the same thing over and over again and expecting different results'. This idea guided me to a personal (and then a business) path of leadership that I call Invoking the Feminine.

We are living in a world that has become increasingly insane in recent centuries, and we currently have no idea as to how we can extract ourselves from this and create a world that is safe, secure and fit for all, rather than just an elite few to live in.

We have suffered at the hands of and been imprisoned by the 'isms' of fascism, jihadism, communism, capitalism and others. These are theologies and philosophies that have been driven or condoned by Masculine-based religious and business models, all of which have led to the creation of weapons of mass destruction and caused the most destructive wars that we have ever known.

The Masculine, a predominantly (but not exclusively) male energy, has ruled the world for tens of thousands of years. In many ways, it has served humankind well. It has stimulated order, discovery, technology, hierarchy and social order. Yes, it has also stimulated war and destruction, but often times of conflict have led to leaps of invention and innovation. It has led us to where we are able to extend our physiological and psychological abilities through technology, out beyond our planet and into the depths of space.

It's values of order, command and control, hierarchy, discipline, rapid response and predominantly logical non-emotional thinking raised us from small nomadic hunter-gatherer tribes to dwellers of the glistening cities of today.

But we have now reached the stage that to continue with this way of thinking will doom us. Allowing the Masculine spirit to remain dominant will no longer serve humanity. The pendulum has reached its full swing and to allow it to swing further will unbalance us all.

At this point in time, focusing on the Masculine only serves an ever smaller and ever more elite group of people (mainly men) who have the power, the money and the means of seizing ever more assets, resources and power at the expense of the other living souls that share the planet.

They increasingly use a perverted (or 'toxic') aspect of the Masculine to control society by instilling it with fear, financial desire and anxiety in equal parts. This enables unprecedented levels of societal control. A small group of male-dominated corporations now controls the finance, the technology, the food resources (even the seeds of our plants), the water resources of the planet, the private details of every person, the ability to wage war when and where it suits them, the communications and media networks, even education.

This emphasis on the Masculine continues its attempts to suppress the Feminine spirit with its creative, connected, networked, synergistic, harmonious and intuitive qualities.

We see this in all aspects of society: from the kidnapping of young girls as sex slaves by Muslim extremist groups to the news of systematic abuse of children by powerful religious and political male leaders on a global scale.

Not only has it actively repressed the flowering of the Feminine, but it has also created and enabled a warped representation of the Masculine as well. Where are the strong male role models, where are the values of responsibility, duty, honour, quiet and protective strength, brotherhood and respect in role models today? Where are today's knights who protect the weak and helpless? Why are greater numbers of young men committing suicide than at any other time? The male role models presented today are overpaid and over-hyped sports stars, soldiers duped into believing they are protecting their country by fighting international wars for dubious political or corporate reasons, or rap stars with misogynistic values. We need to restore the Masculine so that it can be in balance with the Feminine.

Within the business world too, repression of the Feminine continues. Under what justification does 'a glass ceiling' even exist today? How is it still justifiable in any way to pay a woman any less for doing the same job as a man? These are not just 'women's rights' (a classic use of language that can serve to demean or diminish a topic) – these are human rights.

Yet many women in their justifiable desire to actualise themselves, to prove themselves and to forge a career, have had to adapt to a Masculine way of doing business in order to accomplish their dreams. Many others have chosen to reject this in order to fulfil themselves as nurturers and mothers and have suffered for it by virtue of loss of status and career.

We now need to have more women (and men) in positions of power in business and society who embrace the Feminine principles and traits that can lead to global transformation. We must once again, despite the pressure that will be brought to bear on us, come to respect and embrace natural Feminine power and lead with our instinctive Feminine energies to overthrow the exclusive use of Masculine values as measures of success and status in the world today.

As more and more women embrace the spiritual power of the Feminine, it gives more men the permission to embrace their Feminine power too. Already, men are starting to embrace the Feminine by looking within to find meaning and purpose rather than relentlessly pursuing profit, bonuses and status. They are beginning to value experience over ownership and conservation over consumerism.

Why is it so vital that more women and men who embrace the Feminine rise as the leaders of business and society today? The answer is simple: business controls the money, the resources and the future. It dictates where and when wars are fought, where resources are applied, how political leaders act and the urgency with which we act to save our planet.

What is required now is nothing less than the transformation of the world. This must be accomplished through the rise of the Feminine spirit – in all aspects of life, but especially in business. The time of making profits from pain, from scarcity, from suffering and from destroying our planet must end.

The way of *Invoking the Feminine* is the way of making profit from peace, from conservation and from renewal. Why can't there be profit in solving world hunger or in replacing weapons with financial aid?

In order to achieve this, a huge shift is required, nothing less than a revolution in our way of thinking and in our approach to spirituality, energy and values. We need to throw off the shackles of the old Masculine and replace it with the new Feminine; to embrace Feminine-based business, Feminine-based society and Feminine-based faith.

The world has had three key industrial revolutions so far, the last being the communications and ICT revolution. Ironically, it is this that has opened the doors through which the Feminine spirit can rise again, connecting and networking through social media we can now synergise and organise faster than ever before.

Now there is a fourth industrial revolution coming. By the time it is here, the Feminine must be significantly stronger in the world. If it is not, the hold of the elite few will be strengthened further. This new industrial revolution is one of robotics, of genetics, of life sciences and of nanotechnology. We can be certain that these new sciences are already being used for the purposes of waging future wars, of further controlling the population and of securing the hold of those at the top.

Previous industrial revolutions progressively removed the need for manual labour, a costly resource. This new revolution, through the enhancement of AI (artificial intelligence), may very well remove the need for intellectual labour. What value will humanity be afforded then? What will those in power do with all those unemployed ex-professionals?

There is an old story told by Native American people that tells of the People of the Eagle and the People of the Condor. It is said that the People of the Eagle will come to dominate the People of the Condor and to control and repress them, but that a time will come when the People of the Condor will rise again. Eventually the People of the Eagle and of the Condor will live in harmony.

Ultimately, we should seek balance, the Feminine and the Masculine acting in harmony and with mutual respect for the benefit of humanity and all sentient beings on the planet. Only then will humanity rise to meet its full potential, the potential given to it by a Universal Spirit (or the 'Force' for those fans of Star Wars).

I see a new kind of woman and man, strong in Feminine qualities, they have new dreams and visions for the world and the ambition to fulfil them. They build new networks, using influence and leverage and not position to project a new kind of power. They build and empower strong and smarter families, teams, communities and networks. They acknowledge and affirm others and do not second-guess or disempower themselves. They hold their ground, defining the boundaries of their engagements and continuing to invest in their skills and expertise over their lifetimes. They know what they want and act to make it so. They are courageous, acting from the heart despite the fear created by the mind. Like the warrior goddesses of old, they are slow to anger but terrible in their fury. They are holistic in their thinking and foresee consequences, making them powerful catalysts for a new tomorrow. They are transformers – drawn to beauty, to art, to serving others and to life. They are the Feminine, the Perfecting.

The story of *Invoking the Feminine* is told through the tale of a father guiding his daughter as she seeks answers to life's big questions after a tragic loss. Sometimes it takes tragic loss for us to question life and accepted wisdom. Of course, each of us (whether man or woman) is that daughter. We are all seekers of knowledge and guidance as we each search for our own path. This book is a journey through another philosophy; a re-awakening of a spiritual or philosophical path long repressed but not forgotten, a new Invocation of the Feminine.

The story is a journey and as the book progresses and the daughter finds her way towards and reconnects with the Feminine, so too, I hope, will you.

Let the Invocation begin.

Sean Weafer
Dublin, Ireland.

Samhain 2018

1

Prologue

The fluorescent lights of the treatment room hummed softly as the young man sat on the examination table. Next to him was a tall, skinny, bearded man dressed in a white coat, his long hair tied back in a ponytail. He was fumbling with some needles in a small box.

The young man on the table was shirtless, his bare chest and back stuck with long thin needles that jutted from his body as if he were a human porcupine. He winced as the acupuncturist stuck yet another needle in sharply and then twirled it with his long, thin fingers. The action caused a jolt of pain to run through the young man's body and he winced.

"Have you been having any dreams recently?" asked the healer.

The young man looked up at him with a surprised look on his face. "Dreams? Funnily enough, yes I have. One that keeps coming back every night for the last three weeks. How did you know?"

"Just a hunch. Tell me about it."

He was comfortable with this man – a friend he had known for several years. He respected him; not just for his healing abilities – he respected him even more for his esoteric knowledge - and so he happily shared his dream.

"I'm driving out west in Connemara near the lakes, just as twilight is falling. Next thing I know, the car has gone off the road and is sinking into the lake. The last thing I see before the car sinks completely into the dark bog water is this huge monster rising up out of the lake and staring straight at me. It has a long neck and a powerful body. It opens its jaws to show huge, sharp teeth. It rushes through the water towards me, clearly intent on eating me. Knowing it's going to be a horrible ending, I look up into the sky for what is to be my last view of this world and I see the most perfect, bright, full moon rising into the twilight sky. Despite knowing what is rushing towards me and what's going to happen, I am completely awestruck by the absolute beauty of that image. Then the dream ends."

"Interesting. Any idea what it means?" asked the healer.

"Not a clue I just wish it would stop. I've had the same bloody dream for three weeks now."

"But don't you understand what it means?" asked his friend.

"No, should I?"

"Sean, I know your background and your interests. I know you know mine as an initiated witch of the Italian tradition. Are you seriously telling me you can't read what's being communicated to you in the dream?"

"Kevin, I can't interpret it."

"OK, look. As your acupuncturist, I can tell that you were born with a powerful Feminine or Yin energy, which makes you highly intuitive and deeply empathetic, even prophetic. Growing up, you felt and cared deeply for everyone and everything around you. Perhaps more than a young child should.

At some point however, perhaps to protect yourself, you developed a powerful Masculine or Yang energy. You became the warrior spirit that you approach life with today. Everything is a struggle; everything is a battle. You're always alert to potential threats. You've immersed yourself in this through your martial training and your work."

"That deep, dark lake that you sink into is the womb of the Mother, drawing you down into the dark mysteries and secrets of death, rebirth and the unknown. The monster rising from its depths is the awakened power of the Feminine. Once unleashed, if uncontrolled and unfocused it can be a terrible, unstoppable and destructive force capable of devouring all before it but when guided and focused it is an awesome power for change."

"The full moon is the Feminine in all its glory reflecting a softer glow of the sun onto the Earth, the Mother and Healer rising into her ascendancy and power."

The young man listened carefully and reflected on his friend's words, seeing their truth and surprised that he hadn't himself seen the symbolism and patterns woven into the dream himself. "But what does all that mean?"

The healer fixed him with a look. "I believe that the Feminine or the Goddess is reclaiming you for Her own,' he said. 'Returning you to Her path. You will start to rediscover things about yourself, as well as new abilities and feelings. Over time and I don't know how long this will take, the Feminine will grow stronger within you until eventually it is as powerful as your Masculine energies. Once that happens, you will find your path. I believe the Goddess has work for you here."

2

The Parable of the Tree

The father looked out of the window and pointed towards the back of the garden. "What do you see?" he asked his daughter.

"The garden."

"Yes, but what's at the back of the garden?"

The young woman looked again and saw the evergreen trees bathed in the bright sunshine of a beautiful spring day. A shaft of light that shone clearly through the trees blinded her momentarily, and for just a moment she could sense the Earth warming up and renewing, things flourishing within the ground, waiting to bring forth their blossoms in just a few weeks. It was her favourite time of the year, the time when the cherry blossoms would bloom. But she was confused at her father's question, what did he expect her to say?

"Trees?"

"Exactly. Have I ever told you the Parable of the Tree?" asked her father.

"No."

"First, describe to me what you see when you look at the tree?"

"I see branches, leaves, twigs … what's the point here, Dad?"

"What else do you see?"

"Nothing … just what I said…"

"So, you see the leaves, the branches, the trunk of the tree and yet that is not all there is of the tree, is it?" said her father.

"How do you mean?"

"You see what everyone else sees when they look at a tree, the part of the tree that is bathed in light and reaches to the sun for nourishment and life right?"

"Yes."

"But that's not all there is to a tree, is it? A complete tree also has that part of itself that is hidden in the darkness of the Earth, unseen, covered in shadow. And yet this part provides a tree with its stability, its roots and the water and nutrients needed to nourish the tree, it is as important as that part of the tree that we see reaching towards the light. Am I right?"

"Yes…" the daughter said, unsure as to where this particular conversation was going.

"So it is with people," her father continued. "The old traditional Masculine religions teach us that we should focus only on that part of ourselves that is good, that reaches towards the light and that by doing so we shall be 'saved'. They set rules to live by to ensure that we focus on developing that part of ourselves that they deem to be 'good', by their commandments and their rules. They urge us to look to a 'Sky God' and to focus on the perfection to be found in the spirit world not to the Earth or to the physical essence of which we are formed.

They actively discourage anything that is perfectly natural to the birds and the bees, that which has a sexual or an earthly joyful or physical element at all seeking to repress what is the natural life-affirming part of us. They have especially repressed women, the natural balance to the male, the nurturer, and the life-giver. They have painted women as 'fallen' or as temptresses, providing excuses for the continued repression and abuse of women around the world.

"But they choose to ignore completely that humankind has a shadow side that is just as natural to our nature too. A desire not to be controlled by rules but to choose to be free of them; a desire to express our life force through the joy of physical sex and lust, through wine and song, even through the fierce heat of battle or physical competition…

"As I've said before, excess is the enemy of growth and of others. Too much of something is never good. But a healthy respect for and attention to the dual side of our natures is perfectly natural and should be embraced too. When we experience joy, we are truly in the moment of living, allowing our 'selves' to get out of the way and the Universal Soul to pour its energy through us and into manifestation in this world, like removing the built-up resistance conditioned into us by society. The thrill of something illicit, of breaking a rule, of doing something naughty

… is that not also joy and is joy therefore not the highest element of life?

"When we experience joy, at that moment we are in perfect flow with the Universal Soul. We allow all of the energy of the universe that we can channel into the world … it is not restricted by thought or concern or anxieties. The tree is therefore a perfect example of the old saying: 'As above, so below and as below, so above'. Christians would say 'Whatever is loosed in heaven is loosed on Earth, and whatever shall be loosed on Earth shall be loosed in heaven".

The Parable of the Tree is that we are not just one thing or the other but that we have the capability to be one with the infinite potential that is the Universal Soul, the Goddess or God or Force, whatever you choose to call it. That we should work to reach a stage of integration between our higher and lower selves, between our light and our shadow natures, and to respect and explore them both equally, keeping in mind the principle of 'doing unto others as you would have them do unto you'. Only in that way can we become one being both earthly and spiritual, body and soul. A true co-creator in the unfolding of the wonder that is the Universal Soul.

"This is the work of one who walks the way of 'Invoking the Feminine'. Such a person is one of 'the Perfecting'. This is a soul who freely and consciously chooses to work on their development to ensure that they reach their highest potential in a given life. A soul who understands that they cannot and could never be perfect but who still willingly commits themselves to walking the Path of Perfecting. They are committed to finding a balance between the Masculine and the Feminine within themselves, choosing to see the world with different eyes, not through the eyes of those conditioned by old faiths but through eyes that see the glory of the Universal Soul in all things.

A soul who counts every experience, both good and bad, to be of value to themselves, who counts every breath, every word, every act as a prayer of Creation. A soul not limited by the fears, anxieties and insecurities of others but willing and able to engage with the world on their terms, understanding that what they do is always for the greater glory and the manifestation of the Universal Soul in Creation. A soul who serves Creation by accelerating the unfolding of the Universal Soul's infinite potential through their everyday lives.

"This is the life path that I walk sweetheart. This is my way in life and the one that I would love to show you if you would be happy for me to do so. Would you like me to?"

"But Dad, why have you not spoken about this before? Why has this been hidden from me until now?" his daughter asked. "You know how bad I've felt about losing Mom. You know the pain that I suffer every single day. I know you've been doing your best but why not share this with me before this? Why?"

"I suppose my own grief blinded me to yours sweetheart. However, times of loss and grief can also be times of change and great learning, a door to a path that can lead downward to bitterness and recrimination or upwards to hope and new life.

"Long ago I chose to be a part of the Path of Perfecting and in doing so to fulfil the will of the Universe though living my life on my terms and not on the terms of those who would choose to dictate that life to me.

"I have chosen to live my life fearlessly and to seek joy in everything that I do. This is the path that I want to show you now but only if you want it. It is a rebel's path and not one for the fainthearted but it can help you to rise again. If you feel you are ready then I can show you the way now."

3

The Path of the Maiden/Warrior - Bridgid

The father led his daughter up two flights of stairs to what had once been the attic or the loft of the house. This was now his office, to which he often retired, and was a place that his daughter, as a child, had been gently discouraged from entering without his blessing.

She knew the layout of the room, however. It was wood-panelled, with wooden floors and a Persian rug that her father had picked up on his travels in the Middle East. A large plasma TV screen was set into the far wall so that he could indulge his love of movies, and family photos were spread around the room. Her gaze lingered briefly on a recent photo of herself with her mother and her heart lurched. Two easy chairs were placed in the centre of the room, set just back from her father's desk on which was perched his laptop and the usual untidy pile of documents, papers, pens and various technical gadgets. She began to wonder just why she had been brought here.

"Take a seat, sweetheart," the father said, pointing at one of the easy chairs "and make yourself comfortable." Once she was settled in a comfortable chair, her father began to speak.

"First, let me explain what we are about to do. Once I have, then I'll help you experience something of the Way. It's very simple and yet can be very profound. As it is absolutely unique for everyone, it's usually only something that can be taught once someone has started to seek another way in life and spirit. The Way of Invoking the Feminine has three key paths. These paths are called the Path of the Warrior, the Path of the Healer and The Path of the Mystic.

Each path has its own three virtues and it is on these virtues that we focus as we walk 'the path of the Perfecting' which is the journey all the Perfecting are walking, no matter where they may be found in the world.

"So now I'll start the process of taking you through all of the paths. But first, I want to give you just a feel for what you might encounter as we begin the inner journeys that allow you to meet the guardians and archetypes of each of these paths. All of the paths are aligned with the year and their start and end are aligned with the summer and winter solstices and the spring and autumn equinoxes or the movements of the sun and the moon.

"The Path of the Warrior commences at the beginning of winter. It is commonly known today as Halloween or the evening of All Hallows, a Christianised feast day. Before the Christians, we knew it as Samhain in the once-Celtic lands. or the 'time of the dead', when the veils between the seen and the unseen are at their thinnest and we communed with both the dead and the elemental creatures of the land. It is a time when the energy vibrations of this world are at their weakest and those of other worlds and dimensions and their entities and life forms can make an impact here and take shape and form.

It is a time of the eternal struggle for regeneration and also a time of reflection. It is here that we lay the plans for the coming year and prepare ourselves for what is to come. We gather our strength and ready ourselves to recommit to our journey. It is a time when we reflect on death and on our own mortality and on the lives of those who have left us and those who are still with us".

"The form of the guardian of this path is a powerful warrior, for who lives closer to death and transformation every day than a warrior on the battlefield?

"Then, at the mid-winter solstice when the energy of the Earth is at its lowest, usually around December 21st, we start our plans for the year to come. It is then that our focus becomes as finely honed as the sharpest blade. This is the turning of the energies, a time when the energies on the Earth are at their lowest ebb. We celebrate the promise of the future year and the quickening of life as the energies return to breathe life into that which grows within the Earth and which will soon burst out into life and into the returning sun.

"This then leads to the spring equinox, or Imbolc as we know it, usually about February or March. This is the time of the Healer, when the energies of life are returning and growth is in the air. New lambs are born and new life abounds. The energy of the Earth begins to grow stronger and we take advantage of that to bring even more healing and aid to those around us. We city dwellers have lost our connections with the wheels of nature and have become unbalanced and therefore more easily distracted and enslaved because of it.

Bealtine or 'the fires of Baal', in May/June marks the coming of early summer.

Struck with the wonder of life in full flow, we seek to understand its mysteries, yearning to live a life immersed in wonder as though through the eyes of a child, we seek to understand and experience the mystery of life in all its forms. This time, including Lughnasa in August, is the time of the Mystic.

At Lughnasa, the Mystic Path turns to embracing the joy, abundance and blessings in our lives and to seeking to share that with others, even if this means challenging previous beliefs, stereotypes and prejudices.

It is also the time when we begin our reflection in preparation for when we return to the Path of the Maiden or Warrior but this time at a level higher up on the spiral of our personal evolution. Even though it begins the turning of the seasons, there is beauty and majesty in the autumn and joy in seeing the world returning to stillness. Are you with me so far?"

"Yes," the young woman replied brightly. She was starting to enjoy herself now; she had not been too sure what to expect when they had entered the loft, but she was now fascinated by what her father was saying.

"Okay," her father said. "however just understanding something with our mind is one thing - experiencing the path can be quite another. So, I'd like to give you an experience of the first path, that of the Warrior. To do that, we are going to undertake a guided meditation, a journey into your inner mind if you will. All I need you to do is close your eyes and relax.

"It's important to remember that everyone's experience of the path is different. What they see, experience, hear and learn is often a function of where they are in their lives. Every time an experienced 'walker' walks a path, it has usually been preceded by one of the other paths and each path that you walk changes you.

As I said earlier, think about the paths as an ascending spiral. Each time you return to a path, usually months may have passed. It should be that you have travelled upwards through the spiral and are now experiencing the path again but at a higher level of self-understanding. Therefore, the experience, if you have learned the lessons from the previous paths, should be different, as will the challenges and the learning.

It's important to remember that these paths are simply a means of manifesting aspects of the Universal Soul, who speaks to us through our imagination but who sings to us through our emotions. Walking the paths connects us with the Universal Soul in a deep and meaningful way. These are moments when we connect with the energy of the universe, these journeys are actually sacred moments.

Now, close your eyes and let me guide you on this first important journey."

Once the young woman had done so, she heard her father move about the room. Then the most gentle and soothing music started to play. She instantly began to relax as her body unconsciously responded to the rhythm of the music. As she settled herself back in the seat, she heard her father's voice start to speak again. But this time there was something different about it. It was slower and deeper and his rhythm of speaking had changed.

It was not unpleasant, in fact it was very soothing and was helping her to relax deeply and rapidly, her body loosening and settling into the chair. She felt the music wrap itself around her and felt herself letting go and falling into a deeper, more relaxed state. Unbidden images rose up in her mind from the depths of her unconscious.

Suddenly, she found herself on a green and grassy plain. The sun felt warm on her face and there was a swishing sound as the wind moved through the long grasses that surrounded her. Beyond the grass, she saw a high stone wall surrounding a compound. It had tall, strong oaken gates that were open and unguarded. A red pennant flew upon the wall and was snapping in a light, warm breeze. All the grass and trees had been cut away so that a large, cleared area surrounded the compound. As she walked towards it, she felt exposed and a little fearful but she continued walking.

As she entered under the wall and through the open gates she could see a large fire blazing in the centre of the compound. Seated on a large, elaborately carved seat was a woman in a light armoured breastplate that was decorated with a swirling half-moon pattern and precious stones that sparkled in the sun and the firelight. She was beautiful, slim yet toned and muscular, with tanned arms and long, shapely legs and the most beautiful flaming red hair. Apart from the breastplate, she wore only a short skirt-like garment and laced-up sandals. Her body was a perfect specimen of physical, athletic, yet sensual womanhood. Beside her chair leaned a two-handed sword.

As the young woman entered the compound, the Warrior looked up from her contemplation of the fire, smiled at her and beckoned the young woman forward. "Come," she said, motioning to a chair beside her. "Come and sit."

As the young woman sat down, all her fears disappeared. She felt warm and welcomed. The Warrior looked upon her guest and smiled her warm smile again. "You are welcome, young one," she said. "I am honoured to meet you. I know your father well."

"What is this place?" the young woman asked.

"This is the place where you summoned me to meet you," said the Warrior.

"I called you?" said the young woman.

"Yes," said the Warrior simply. "This place is within your imagination, your inner landscape. It is here that I can transcend the boundaries of space and time in which your world is bound. Here we are nowhere and yet somewhere both in time and out of it and it is all of your making. Here is where I can take shape and form in order to be of service to you and guide you. This is a sacred space and it is unique and different for each person who comes to me. I can even change shape and form and gender to one that is most relevant to my visitor."

"So, this is not your true form?" asked the young woman. "It is, for you," said the Warrior, "but it may be different for others. It is simply the form most appropriate for our meeting. However, you are welcome here and I am here to help with your questions. So, what would you ask of me?"

The young woman thought for a moment as she looked at this beautiful, powerfully capable and potentially ferocious woman. She had no doubt that the Warrior possessed a strength of mind and body that far surpassed her own or that of any person she had ever met. She appeared capable, intelligent, and warm but also deadly and somehow 'more than' a person. What it was that made the Warrior so powerful, the young woman could not quite fathom.

As she reflected on this, she realised she was being watched in return. She noticed that the warrior had a great stillness about her. She appeared relaxed yet capable of powering into action should the need arise. She seemed very aware both of her physical self and of her surroundings; perfectly comfortable and at ease yet grounded and very physical, even sensual, uncomfortably so for the young woman, who found herself feeling awkward seated next to this powerful Feminine warrior.

The young woman still wanted to understand the purpose of this visit and why her father had 'sent' her here. She resolved to learn as much as she could on this visit and on any subsequent visits to the path. "Can you tell me about the Perfecting?" she asked eventually.

Without hesitation, the Warrior began to speak. "The Perfecting are the path walkers of the Feminine. They are the souls who have committed themselves to the unfolding of their personal power and potential. They are aware of their immortality, of being able to live through many lives. They understand that death is not an ending but a portal, a dimensional change, an entrance to another vibrational level of existence. They do not limit themselves to the rule or limitations of your world but seek rather to find the ways and experiences by which they can accelerate their soul's evolution both in the service of themselves and others.

They realise that your world is not ruled by the spiritually strong, hence the condition of your world, as base emotions rule there and not the higher emotions that we strive for on the path. The Deceivers have created a world of fear and of base emotions and lower energies from which they feed and gain sustenance."

"So, what and who are you, then?"

"I am the Warrior, known also as the Maiden and I am the first of the three guardians and custodians of the Path. I represent the body and the physical things of life; I represent wealth and career, the pure manifestation of energy in its most dense form. I am sometimes known as the Morrigan. I also represent change and death for as the body grows older it changes inexorably and reminds us that time on your plane is limited and must be used wisely. The sword is my symbol and the crows and ravens my creatures."

With that, she suddenly stood, her body moving like a big cat, swift, silent and sure. She seized the two-handed sword beside her chair and swung it effortlessly and with the practised movement of one who is intimately connected with an object. As she moved, turning and spinning effortlessly, the sword moved in a blur around her, flashing both in the sunlight and the reflected glow of the flames from the fire. She held it effortlessly and moved it as if it were an extension of her body. She danced around the fire and then finished her demonstration with a shout and a thrust of the sword into the air. For a moment she stood still and unmoving. Magnificent. In that moment, the young woman understood that she was in the presence of a power aspect of the Universal Soul.

Sitting again, the Warrior continued. "The sword is associated with violence and war. But the sword is only an implement, a tool. What decides its purpose is the intention of the person who uses it. It can be used to kill or to swiftly and cleanly cut off corrupting flesh. It can be used to end the unnecessary suffering of another or to protect the weak and empower those of courage to act. So it is with a life. It is measured by the intentions of the soul who has been granted that life. To live that life to the full, there are three elements to the Warrior path.

"The first of those elements is that of Self-Discipline, or the ability to see things to which you have committed yourself through to the end, despite the odds that you face or the distractions of the wider world. For distraction is what the Deceivers want. They are dark entities who do not wish you to achieve your full potential, to accomplish the union with the Universal Soul that is the birth right of all who are born onto your plane of existence.

Self-discipline challenges their power and control, preventing them from feeding off the lower energy vibrations created through greed, the lust for power, hatred, fear and want. They do not possess the power of love, or of hope or of selflessness, and it is these energies that starve them of power and life. The higher energies destroy them. They would rather see the universal power and force within you, your power to make change, to create and to evolve, just wasted or dispersed. They do not want their status quo challenged or questioned. They do not want a world of enlightened people or truly powerful individuals who have awakened to their deceptions and who's combined, raised energy begins to raise the higher powers within the world.

Hence the distractions of life, the promotion of a world where people are pressured to achieve 'success' without ever really understanding or defining it. You are programmed from birth to consume and then consume more. New toys and new distractions are endlessly created to fuel the need to buy. But all this fuels is slavery, slavery through distraction. The Deceivers want you to give up, to be distracted, to conform and not to focus on the power of the Universal Soul that lies within us. This is a power to accomplish not just success but greatness, a greatness that allows more of the Universal Soul to manifest in the world.

Building self-discipline allows us to fight the distractions and keeps us on an even course. It helps us to overcome the fear and even the shame we feel when we go against the status quo or do not measure up to the false standards of a society that cause us to question or doubt ourselves.

All warriors must cultivate self-discipline: the ability to say no to oneself so that one may reach an objective, learn a skill, develop a relationship, evolve, become noble. The self-discipline of deferment and of practice, sometimes the submission of oneself and one's desires for the greater good of others. This is how warriors walk the path of Perfecting.

The second element of the Warrior path is that of Courage, the ability to act and make change; not just in the absence of fear, but particularly when fear is present in all its forms. Fear is the enemy that is conquered first by your imagination and then by your will. It is the one thing that limits a life robbing it of its potential and glory. Fear is something that only the courageous can push through. When your fear is mastered, the soul becomes a true channel for the energy of the Universal Soul to manifest its blessings.

Fear is a tool of control too. It limits us. Fear is present every day in every way in your world. That is the victory of the Deceivers, that is why they control your world. They make you fearful of life, about money, your relationships, and your self-esteem. They create fear and inject it into your world in many ways. The Deceivers have mastered the art of fear and they subtly blend it through their vassals into your media, your politics and even your entertainment. They create fear of many things, 'the others', scarcity, war, minorities. It is a fear that destroys individuals and splits families and communities. Or they create anxiety about life in general. What is worse is when they manage to get you to fear yourself, your power, your ability and your uniqueness?

That fear is first created when they isolate and separate people from each other. Is it not strange that in your world of networked and instant communications, people are more isolated and fearful than ever? This is what the Perfecting stand against.

The third part of the path, then, is Service to others.

There is no greater thing than service to others, even to the extent of sacrificing oneself in the just defence of others, such as a warrior might do. To give your life for that of another is the greatest of service. Service requires all of the qualities of a warrior, self-sacrifice, courage, discipline, a willingness to subjugate yourself and your own desires for the greater good. Service is connected to the purest of love.

While many would do all of these things for those that they love, to willingly serve for the benefit of a stranger in need, that is the purest love of all. Why? Because it demonstrates an understanding of that which connects you all, that you are all indivisible as a part of the Universal Soul that any and all service to others is ultimately in service to yourself and the walking of your path.

This is the secret of defeating the power of the Deceivers. Service to others creates positive energies and emotions in the world. It starts to replace the baser energies on which they feed. Starve them and they will loosen the bonds of slavery upon you."

The young woman listened in astonishment, but even before she had fully processed what she had heard, the Warrior stood abruptly and spoke again.

"My time here with you is done for now. In the future if you need me then just call my name, Bridgid. You may call to me at any time, for I am always here for you. I always watch over you. Remember this place, for it will be easier to visit here when you are alone and on the path. Until our next meeting, my sister, go with good fortune."

As the young woman began to protest, the images faded until she saw only the darkness inside her closed eyes. Unwilling to leave the memory of the meeting, she waited a few moments before opening her eyes to see her father looking at her with a smile on his face.

"Here," he said, "have this." as he handed her a beautifully bound hardcover book with her name embossed in red and gold on the front cover.

"This is where you can log your journeys and your messages. It is unique to you. Over time, as you review it, you will see the patterns of your life take shape and see the messages that the Universal Soul shares with you to create your life as a part of the Perfecting. It is here you can record your journey on the path and your conversations and lessons from the Feminine part of the Universal Soul. This is where we start to bring more of the Feminine into the world and gradually build the resistance against the power of the Deceivers."

He smiled. "Welcome to the Perfecting, sweetheart."

4

The Path of the Mother/Healer - Epona

The late spring sunshine had dimmed and the early evening shadows had lengthened when the young woman again ascended the staircase to her father's study.

This time, before she sat in the chair, she noticed that he was lighting a green candle. When she asked him about it, he told her that the paths had different colours. The Warrior's, or Maiden's path was Red. This was the colour of energy, prosperity and battle. When he said this, she remembered the red pennant snapping in the breeze when she had met the Maiden. He explained that the path of the Healer, or the Mother, was the green path of healing and of blossoming nature. The path of the Mystic (or Wise Woman or Crone) was purple. This was the colour of nobility and spirit.

The father had also lit incense. His daughter had not noticed it the first time, as she had been overwhelmed by her first experience of visiting a path. "Why the incense?" she asked.

"When entering the sacred space where you meet the aspects of the

Feminine, it can be helpful to create music, visuals and even smells that relate to the aspect of the Feminine that you wish to connect with.

Ritual magicians call these 'correspondences' as they align your unconscious and your spirit with the vibration or the frequency of the spell that they wish to carry out and in the case of dark magic, the Deceiver or demon they wish to invoke. We apply the same rules when accessing the Feminine aspect of the Universal Spirit. Now, just sit back, relax and close your eyes."

As his daughter did so, her father turned on the soothing and restful music again. This time she found herself falling into the relaxed state much more quickly, sure in the knowledge that wherever she went it would be safe.

This time she found herself in a small cottage, warm and cosy. The experience of the path felt even more real to her. To her amazement there was even a gorgeous smell of something cooking in an old iron cauldron hanging on the open fire. Herbs of all kinds grew in window boxes and on shelves neatly positioned around the spacious room. Everything seemed neat and ordered.

As she looked out of the small window, the first things that caught her attention were the many beautiful horses grazing contentedly in paddocks around the cottage. The sun shone down through flowering oak and ash and hazel trees, casting a dappled light onto the beautifully tended garden in front of the cottage.

Further away, she saw a large lake with a wind whipping up small white waves on its surface. White clouds scudded by in a bright blue sunny sky. Beyond it were mountains with white-topped peaks reaching up into the sky. Animals of all kinds, from the most exotic to the most domesticated, roamed the grounds outside the cottage. She stared wide-eyed and open-mouthed as a huge animal which reminded her of an ancient dinosaur stretched its long neck and its humped back out of the lake and then dived back into the dark depths with a giant splash.

She turned on hearing the sound of boots walking briskly on the stone floor of the cottage. Entering the room from a hallway was a very attractive mature woman. She was dressed in a tailored white blouse, a jade neck scarf, black riding breeches that highlighted her figure, highly polished black riding boots and black gloves. She had a lovely face and her figure, while not as slender or muscular as the Warrior's, was nonetheless very sensual and physical. She had a warm smile and an aura of power and radiated loving and relaxed acceptance. It was as if she blossomed with life.

"Welcome,' she said, "to my humble home. Please sit." she said as she waved an elegant hand at an armchair placed near the fireplace. There was a lovely smell coming from the fire. The smell was not just of the vegetable stew that was bubbling in the cauldron but came from the fire itself, a combination of burning peat mixed with herbs. The young woman felt immediately safe and at peace in this space.

The woman sat in a matching armchair and crossed her booted feet onto a small footstool in front of her. She seemed perfectly at ease and relaxed in her surroundings and smiled gently at the younger woman. "I believe that you have already met my sister?" she said.

"The Warrior is your sister?"

"Indeed. As well as being an aspect of myself, of course. We three are a trinity powerful individually but together a formidable combination of the Universal Soul. And please, you may call me Epona, my dear. It is only one of my many names, but I quite like it. How do you like my humble home?" While she spoke, she reached out and took a well-worn and dark brown staff from near the fireplace. She rested it over her legs and placed both her hands on it.

"It is beautiful. Do you live here alone?"

The woman seemed genuinely puzzled by the question and arched an eyebrow before responding. "Alone? I am never alone. Neither are you. We are all connected to the Universal Soul. You simply have to look within to find any and all comfort and companionship that you may need. Everything around you is an image of yourself. If the external is not what you desire, then change the internal. If ever you seek forgiveness from another, forgive yourself first. All are a part of you. If ever you seek salvation, then look within yourself first." She shook her head gently. "There is so much that you have to learn." she said, smiling.

"My child, the Wheel of Ages turns and there is a new time coming but it is important that humanity learns some fundamental lessons first. For this to happen, someone must carry the message to others. It is particularly important that my message and that of my sisters is carried to the rich and the powerful of your world as much as anyone else. Not all are yet possessed by the Deceivers, so there is still hope.

They and everyone in your world must learn that you cannot move to the next level or reach communion with other worlds, spiritual planes and dimensions until you can evolve the Earth into a global and peaceful society. You will not get there by continuing to be fooled by the lies of the Deceivers and their allies and the illusion that the values of conflict, hierarchy, supremacy and profit at any cost are acceptable.

You will not get there while you continue to defile the world around you. Not while you chop down my trees and despoil my rivers, lakes and great seas. Nor while you poison yourselves, your children and my beloved creatures. How many have died already, never to be a living essence again and all in the name of money and profit? How many mountains have been levelled and landscapes submerged in the pursuit of worldly power and possession? When will you learn that life is not about possessing things and owning things? That you cannot find redemption in ownership, that ownership is at best transitory? That you cannot take 'things' on your spiritual journey?

Life is about experiences. You live in a world, of all of the created worlds, that is perfect for experiences. Life abounds here with food, love, sex, pleasure, and pain. This is why a soul comes here to grow itself through experiences. The most enlightened of souls is the one that is forged through experiences."

She paused for a moment looking carefully at the young woman as if to check that she understood her. "To create an enlightened world that can evolve, you have to learn to embrace the values of experiencing life through seeking harmony, synergy, compassion, empowerment, acceptance of difference and empathy. Of these values, the most important are Harmony, Compassion and Empowerment. Let me explain, for that is why you are here.

Harmony is when we seek synergy with others. To find a way for others to be respected and understood despite the fact that they may be different from you. All sentient, enlightened and free beings feel and empathise. What is important is that we can make a space for them to be heard by creating a space of silence within ourselves. You should experience it all. Learn to reflect, rather than reflex when you feel challenged by the thoughts and ideas and ways of others despite the fact that they may be uncomfortable or even fearful."

The young woman listened carefully and intently, knowing that this visit would be as fleeting as the last and wanting to soak up what was coming to her from the Mother. She knew now that she could return any time to the place of visitation but also knew that each time she visited would be unique and different. This was why, after her visit to the Warrior, she had written down everything she had remembered of her words and wisdom. She would do the same when she had returned from this visit.

"Your world is in need of healing," the Mother continued. "There is great and unnecessary suffering caused as a result of the Deceivers and their interference. They feed off human suffering and seek to continue doing so, satisfying their lust for blood from the wars, the orphans and the lost. But remember that such healing cannot come without Compassion, the ability to empathise and feel for others and then act. This is a great and wonderful human gift, the ability to feel for others, to understand their pain. To make a free and conscious decision to help change things is truly the divine aspect of humanity, that piece of you through which the Universal Soul sings.

It is a great and higher energy, an energy that truly ennobles a being and it is poison to the Deceivers and their kind. They loathe it with a passion and seek to remove it from your society.

However, remember that compassion is not pity. It is not something just given away and then forgotten about to ease your own discomfort. Compassion requires that you engage with another's suffering and pain and, through a Warrior's courage, endure with them until they can walk their path unaided.

But beware also. There are those who would trap you in this space.

Has your father ever warned you of 'psychic vampires'? Yes? Those people who would present their suffering for you to heal and then feed off your energies until you yourself have been dragged down to their level? Despite your efforts, they will never change, they too are like the Deceivers, living off the energies of their fellow humans. Be vigilant and remove them, for they are like leeches. They are empty vessels that never seek to change as long as they can find another host.

All of your interactions should help others to reach their own power. You empower others by helping them to stand on their own feet, by helping them discover and align the power, majesty and the bounty of the Universal Soul and claim their unique part of it. You should help others to understand that all of their answers begin and end with their unique and spiritual selves. The Creator has provided everything for you to rise". She paused for a moment as if reflecting on something and then said, "Come with me for a moment would you?"

With that, the woman stood and crossed to the window, her figure now framed in the light. The young woman had not noticed before, but the Mother/Healer was tall.

The Mother turned and beckoned to the young woman and then pointed out of the window. "Do you see out there, at that patch of the garden to the left?"

The young woman looked and saw that on the extreme left of the cottage garden was a small patch that was untended and overrun with weeds, stinging nettles and tall grass.

"Do you see the stinging nettles?" said the Healer.

"Yes", said the young woman, wincing with a painful reminder of when she had fallen into a patch of nettles as a child. She remembered having cream rubbed into her stings by her mother and felt a lump catch in her throat.

"Easy, child. I had not meant to cause you pain only to help you understand that empowerment comes through an active balance. Look beside the nettles. What do you see?"

Beside the nettles were some weeds, flowering with broad, dark green leaves.

"Dock leaves," she said.

"Exactly," said the Healer. "Once stung, the pain of the nettle sting can be eased through crushing dock leaves and rubbing them onto the sting. You know this from when you were but a child."

"Yes." said the young woman, remembering how her father had immediately applied the crushed dock leaves onto her raw arms and legs as soon as he had lifted her out of the patch, stinging his own self badly in the act of protecting his child.

"Empowerment through balance. Just as in nature, all that you need is provided for you to rise. All that is required is that you open your eyes and see. It is the work of enlightened souls to heal those who have been blind so that they can see and then choose their own path to the Great Soul."

The Mother opened her arms. "Come to me, child," she said. The young woman walked up to her and was enfolded in the warmest of hugs she had felt for a long time, filled with love, warmth and safety. The Mother smelled of flowers and earth, of safety and comfort. Reluctantly, the young woman let go and stood back to look at the older woman.

"The time has come for us to part, but as you know, only for now," the Healer said, smiling softly. 'Be strong and brave and live the life that you have to the full. Never feel guilty for living a life to its full potential. We will meet again soon."

With that, the young woman's eyes flickered open and she was once more in the attic room with her father. His eyes were both concerned and loving and it was some time before she forgot the warmth of the Mother's embrace.

5

The Path of the Crone/Mystic - Danu

The cavern was dark, so dark that the young woman couldn't see her hand in front of her face. Even so, she could sense its huge size stretching out in front of her and way above her into a vast space above her head. She caught herself on the edge of panic. She had never been comfortable with dark spaces and now she was in one of the blackest of them all.

Gradually she noticed a faint light up ahead and moved towards it. On reaching it, she found herself in a huge underground space lit with thousands of torches that were fitted into deep cups in the rock. The torches spat and snapped in a wind that teased the flames but seemed to touch nothing else and could be felt nowhere else in the cavern.

In the centre of the cavern was a circle cut into the stone floor. In the centre of the circle was a large black dot. Within the dot there sat what looked like a throne, wonderfully decorated and mounted on a stepped platform.

At first, the throne looked as if it was coloured a dark purple but then she noticed that it was not the throne itself that was purple but the robes of a seated and hunched figure, one completely wrapped in the robe while a cowl hid its face. The young woman felt a stab of fear run through her as the shape within the robe started to move. She remembered that her father had warned her that this visit might be different. He had said that the face of the Wise Woman or the Crone was always covered at first. When revealed, it could show the face of a kind and benevolent old woman or the face of a murderous and terrible hag.

This was why approaching the Wise Woman had to be handled with care. The young woman's father had insisted that she had showered and bathed before this visit. Then she had rubbed an oil that he had given her onto her body and had worn a light dress for the meditation. At first, it had seemed foolish. After all, she was only going on a journey into her imagination. But her father had stopped her complaints with a raised hand.

"Everything we do has a resonance in the world," he had said. "Every thought and every action that we have and take in this world echoes in the next and in every world beyond. You may think you are just imagining these visits," he had said to her, "but they have a reality within yourself and with the Cosmos as a whole on every plane."

Slowly, the hooded figure raised its head until it was staring directly at her. She felt its gaze on her, malevolent, fierce and dangerous. Suddenly she realised that this was not a power to take lightly and that if it chose, she could be wiped from existence by a simple thought of this terrible and powerful being. Her fears grew. But then there was a subtle change.

She felt it in the air around her, which seemed suddenly to have changed from an ominous chill to a kind of warmth that enveloped her. She looked again at the figure, which had reached up two ancient and almost skeletal hands and was removing its hood, pulling it back to reveal its face. But it was not the face of the terrible and vicious hag she had feared but that of a wise old woman, imperious yet kind. The Mystic smiled at her.

"Greetings, my dear, I am known in your world as Danu or sometimes Danann" she said. "and you are most welcome. My sisters have spoken well of you. They say you are a fitting guest and a credit to your father, a noble consort of the Feminine. There is no need to fear. While it's true that there is an aspect of me that is terrible and fearsome to behold or to anger, this is true for all beings. We are all both light and dark, it is the ability to respect and integrate both of these sides that is the never-ending struggle of life."

The old woman stood up and with a surprisingly light step came down from the platform and walked towards the young woman. She exuded imperial majesty and presence. Nothing of her kindly appearance could take away from the raw and terrible power that came from her. This was the aspect of the Feminine that had reached its zenith. This was the aspect of the Feminine who guarded the portal to other worlds.

"My sisters, who you met before me, are the faces of the body and the mind/heart. I am the face of the spirit and of emotion. I complete the trinity of the Feminine and my symbol is that of the rose". As she said the words the cavern suddenly seemed full of the most beautiful scent the young woman had ever known. "The rose has always represented the seekers after truth and the power of love and passion. Now, I am here to complete the lessons of my sisters, so follow me child."

With that, the old woman walked gracefully towards the wall of the cavern and the young woman followed obediently. Here, the rough rock had been chiselled away. On a smooth surface were carved three words almost as if the words were part of the living rock.

The young woman gazed at the words on the wall. She noticed that the words themselves had been inlaid with gold and that the metal shone in the light of the torches, seeming to dance and move with a life of their own. The words were:

Understanding
Purpose
Meaning

The Wise Woman pointed at each of them in turn. "These are the last of the nine values that you must learn and embrace to become truly alive, to become your true self.

I can speak only of the first to you, for the others are so unique, so special to you and to you alone that what they mean will resonate within your soul only if you seek their meaning for yourself. I cannot help you with them. But the first, that of Understanding, that I can guide you on. It requires that you are willing to challenge everything you have ever known or accepted. To learn understanding is to begin the tireless pursuit of truth and knowledge, the real knowledge hidden behind all the shadows, images and mirages that are conjured up to distract you from the reality of the world.

You must know, my dear, that once there was a time when the Feminine was powerful. There was a time when those who served both the Feminine and the Masculine energies were bonded in harmony, each the consort of the other.

On the Earth there reigned peace and bounty for all. Humankind lived in harmony and balance with the world and all the creatures it shared sentience with. But then the envious eyes of the Deceivers saw this world and they came to your realm to dominate, to conquer and to feed. They entered into your world through those they enslaved with the promise of power and wealth, for even then there were those who were but children to the world of the spirit, who had become unbalanced by their desires for the physical world and had begun to turn away from the spirit.

Through the Deceivers their desires became base and warped. Their desire for power grew and with it the suffering they visited among their fellows. The entry of deliberate suffering into the world, the deliberate and calculated creation of loss, fear, injury, pain, dissatisfaction, envy and the baser emotions was encouraged and manipulated by the Deceivers. With the growth of these emotions, the power of the Deceivers and their allies grew. Naturally aligned with the Masculine, the Deceivers created an imbalance in the power and used it to crush the Feminine. Then began the active persecution of women. Then began the aeons of tears as women were seen as the enemy.

The Deceivers rightly feared the power of a resurgent Feminine. It would restore the balance to the world. It had to be repressed.

Temples to and the faiths of the Feminine were sought and destroyed all over the Earth. Servants of the Feminine, men and women, were hunted down, tortured, burned and killed. Women, natural heirs to the power of the Feminine, were degraded mentally, physically and spiritually. Priestesses and wise women were killed, as were wise men and shamans. New religions raised the image of the Masculine and removed that of the Feminine. They were allowed to grow to dominance.

Within these new faiths was the power to control women, their beliefs, their sexuality, their value and their self-worth.

Even worse was that in time, women too came to believe these false lies and untruths about themselves. Literally beaten and battered, they submitted and lost their belief in the Feminine. Stereotypes were created, laws enacted, social conventions established for one purpose and one purpose only, to destroy and remove any trace of the Feminine.

Men too were taught to ignore their finer feelings and that the warrior class was supreme. That violence could solve all problems and that compassion; love and mercy were things of weakness with no place in the society of men. They were taught that competition, dominance, power and profit were the only values that defined a man and his existence. It continues today and that is why the Masculine of today is a warped and pale comparison of the true Masculine.

But the Feminine is once more rising and nothing can stop it. It is the way of Creation that all things come in cycles. Even men are once again discovering the Feminine within themselves, turning away from their baser selves and seeking their own understanding, purpose and meaning, moved to find a better way for all, to find balance within themselves. My sisters and I are here for them too. The Feminine exists not just for her daughters but also for her sons. The balance shall be restored.

Understanding requires challenge; requires questions. It requires effort and it will draw the eyes and the attention of those who would do you harm. It requires courage." The Crone paused for a short moment and then asked; "Have you courage, my child?"

"I don't know," the young woman replied slowly, unsure of what to say in the face of this new knowledge. "What can I do? I'm only one person."

"One person indeed, that is true. But you are bonded by spirit and energy to millions more in your world, millions of other people, male and female, who are also looking for a new way and the rebirth of a time of peace and light. A time free of the darkness, free of the Deceivers, when humanity will once again be benevolent and caring guardians of your world. You are not alone, child.

You simply have not sent your voice out into the world to gather those around you. There is but one question you must ask." With this, the old woman's face came closer to her, so close that the warmth and surprisingly fresh smell of her breath came to rest on the young woman's face. The young woman closed her eyes, a little fearful and unsure of what to expect. The Mystic drew even closer, leaning against her. The old woman's mouth was close to her ear.

"Have you the courage to face your fears? Have you the courage to seize your destiny and forge your life on your terms? Will you walk this noble path with all its tribulations and tears? Have you the courage to be a voice and a light-bringer in the darkness of ignorance? Can you be a strong arm to aid those who would walk this path also? Are you ready to embrace the Feminine in all its wonder and to play your part in bringing balance to the world?

"So, my love, have you the courage to *arise and awaken?*"

When the young woman opened her eyes to answer, she was once more in her father's study.

40

TO BE CONTINUED

About the Author

Sean Weafer is an international executive coach, trainer and conference speaker, specialising in communications in leadership and sales.

He believes that business and personal leadership is genderless and that real leadership is when both men and women can embrace the positive values, energies and traits of the Feminine and the Masculine together and live from a place of balance.

Sean's belief is that it's no longer enough to have reflexive Masculine values as the dominant values in our world. Now we must learn to respect, include and use more reflective Feminine values and that by honouring the Feminine more fully in the world we can rebalance (and ultimately, save) business, society and our planet.

Sean started his career first as a marine engineer and merchant navy officer, worked as a professional bodyguard and then as a sales professional in the tech industry. Along the way he qualified as a psychotherapist and analytical hypnotherapist and now works as a business author, trainer, coach and conference speaker.

He is a life-long student of mysticism and the Celtic spirituality of his childhood in the West of Ireland, where he experienced the pre-Christian beliefs of the rural communities. He has explored beliefs as diverse as Freemasonry, Kabbalistic magic and witchcraft. He has also trained as a past life regression therapist, a Scalar Pranic energy healer and holds a 4th (Yon Dan) degree black belt in the Japanese martial art of Ninpo Taijutsu.

His interests include martial arts, fitness, horse riding, film and photography, historical fiction, travel and a glass or three of nice wine. He lives in Dublin, Ireland with his wife Sharon, their two sons Nicholas and Gregory and their dog Kai.

You can reach him and share your thoughts on the book with him at sean@seanweafer.com